Teacher Reference Handbook

Glencoe McGraw-Hill

Math Connects

Concepts, Skills, and Problem Solving

Course 2

McGraw Hill Glencoe

About the Cover

Nothing beats the thrill of a water slide! Next time you are at a water park, think about math. The water slide is exciting because there is a big vertical drop in a small horizontal distance. In math, that is expressed as a ratio $\frac{\text{rise}}{\text{run}}$, which is called *slope*. You'll learn more about slope in Chapter 6.

Cover image photographed on location courtesy Busch Gardens/Adventure Island, Tampa, Florida. Credit Richard Hutchings.

About the Graphics

Twisted torus. Created with *Mathematica*

A torus with rose-shaped cross section is constructed. Then the cross section is rotated around its center as it moves along a circle to form a twisted torus. For more information, and for programs to construct such graphics, see: www.wolfram.com/r/textbook.

 Glencoe

The *McGraw-Hill* Companies

Send all inquiries to:
Glencoe/McGraw-Hill
8787 Orion Place
Columbus, OH 43240-4027

ISBN: 978-0-07-888884-7
MHID: 0-07-888884-0

Printed in the United States of America.

3 4 5 6 7 8 9 10 006 16 15 14 13 12 11 10 09

Teacher Reference Handbook

Contents

Scope and Sequence

Number and Operations

Whole Numbers

	PreK	Kindergarten	Grade 1	Grade 2	Grade 3	Grade 4	Grade 5	Course 1	Course 2	Course 3	Pre-Algebra	Algebra 1	Geometry
One-to-one correspondence	●	●	●	●	●	●	●						
Count, read, write, name, rename, represent — Numbers to 10	●	●	●	●	●	●	●						
Numbers to 30		●	●	●	●	●	●						
Numbers to 100			●	●	●	●	●						
Numbers to 1,000				●	●	●	●						
Numbers to 10,000					●	●	●						
Numbers to 1 million						●	●						
Numbers to billions							●						
Skip count			●	●	●	●	●						
Equivalent Forms (word, expanded, standard)	●	●	●	●	●	●	●	●					
Place value		●	●	●	●	●	●	●	●				
Powers and exponents								●	●	●	●	●	●
Negative-integer exponents										●	●	●	
Scientific notation										●	●		
Round whole numbers			●	●	●	●	●	●					
Compare and order whole numbers		●	●	●	●	●	●	●					
Represent on a number line		●	●	●	●	●	●	●					
Even and odd numbers, doubles			●	●	●	●	●						
Factors and multiples					●	●	●	●	●	●	●	●	
Prime and composite numbers							●	●	●	●	●	●	
Prime factorization							●	●	●	●	●	●	

● Introduce   ● Develop   ● Reinforce   ● Maintain and Apply   ● Prerequisite Skills

	PreK	Kindergarten	Grade 1	Grade 2	Grade 3	Grade 4	Grade 5	Course 1	Course 2	Course 3	Pre-Algebra	Algebra 1	Geometry
Greatest common factor (GCF)							◐	●	●	●	●	●	
Least common multiple (LCM)							●	●	●	●	●		
Perfect squares, cubes, roots								◐	●	●	●	●	●

Fractions

	PreK	Kindergarten	Grade 1	Grade 2	Grade 3	Grade 4	Grade 5	Course 1	Course 2	Course 3	Pre-Algebra	Algebra 1	Geometry
Model fractional parts of a whole, of a set or group	●	●	◐	●	●	●	●	●	●	●			
Read and write fractions		●	◐	●	●	●	●	●	●	●	●	●	●
Represent fractions on a number line				◐	◐	●	●	●	●	●	●	●	●
Compare and order fractions				◐	◐	●	●	●	●	●	●	●	●
Equivalent fractions					◐	●	●	●	●	●	●	●	●
Simplify fractions					●	◐	●	●	●	●	●	●	●
Least common denominator (LCD)						◐	●	●	●	●	●	●	●
Reciprocal, multiplicative inverse								◐	●	●	●	●	●
Mixed numbers and improper fractions						◐	●	●	●	●	●	●	●
Relate fractions and decimals					●	◐	●	●	●	●	●	●	●

Decimals

	PreK	Kindergarten	Grade 1	Grade 2	Grade 3	Grade 4	Grade 5	Course 1	Course 2	Course 3	Pre-Algebra	Algebra 1	Geometry
Model decimals					●	◐	●	●	●	●	●	●	●
Read and write decimals					◐	●	◐	●	●	●	●	●	●
Represent decimals on a number line						◐	●	●	●	●	●	●	●
Compare and order decimals						◐	●	●	●	●	●	●	●
Round decimals						◐	●	●	●	●	●	●	●
Terminating and repeating decimals								◐	●	●	●	●	●
Non-repeating decimals/ irrational numbers												◐	●

Scope and Sequence

Number and Operations

Ratio, Rate, Proportion

	PreK	Kindergarten	Grade 1	Grade 2	Grade 3	Grade 4	Grade 5	Course 1	Course 2	Course 3	Pre-Algebra	Algebra 1	Geometry
Concept of a ratio							●	●	●	●	●	●	●
Model ratios							●	●	●	●	●	●	●
Read and write ratios							●	●	●	●	●	●	●
Relate ratios to fractions							●	●	●	●	●	●	●
Rates							●	●	●	●	●	●	●
Unit rate							●	●	●	●	●	●	●
Rate of change								●	●	●	●		●
Direct variation								●	●	●	●	●	
Ratio and probability								●	●	●	●	●	
Solve proportions							●	●	●	●	●	●	●
Proportional reasoning							●	●	●	●	●	●	●
Scale drawings								●	●	●	●	●	●
Scale factor								●	●	●	●	●	●
Similar figures							●	●	●	●	●	●	●
Indirect measurement								●	●	●	●	●	●
Dilations											●		●

Percent

	PreK	Kindergarten	Grade 1	Grade 2	Grade 3	Grade 4	Grade 5	Course 1	Course 2	Course 3	Pre-Algebra	Algebra 1	Geometry
Concept of percent, model							●	●	●	●	●		
Relate fractions and decimals to percents							●	●	●	●	●		
Percent of a number							●	●	●	●	●		
Percent one number is of another								●	●	●	●		
Percent proportion $\left(\dfrac{P}{B} = \dfrac{R}{100}\right)$								●	●	●	●		

● Introduce ● Develop ● Reinforce ● Maintain and Apply ● Prerequisite Skills

	PreK	Kindergarten	Grade 1	Grade 2	Grade 3	Grade 4	Grade 5	Course 1	Course 2	Course 3	Pre-Algebra	Algebra 1	Geometry
Percent equation ($RB = P$)								●	●	●	●		
Percent of change								●	●	●	●		
Interest, profit, discount								●	●	●	●		

Integers

	PreK	Kindergarten	Grade 1	Grade 2	Grade 3	Grade 4	Grade 5	Course 1	Course 2	Course 3	Pre-Algebra	Algebra 1	Geometry
Concept of integers, negative numbers							●	●	●	●	●	●	●
Read and write integers							●	●	●	●	●	●	●
Represent on a number line							●	●	●	●	●	●	●
Compare and order integers							●	●	●	●	●	●	●
Absolute value								●	●	●	●	●	●

Rational Numbers

	PreK	Kindergarten	Grade 1	Grade 2	Grade 3	Grade 4	Grade 5	Course 1	Course 2	Course 3	Pre-Algebra	Algebra 1	Geometry
Identify and simplify rational numbers								●	●	●	●	●	●
Represent on a number line								●	●	●	●	●	●
Relate rational numbers to decimals								●	●	●	●	●	●
Compare and order rational numbers								●	●	●	●	●	●

Real Numbers

	PreK	Kindergarten	Grade 1	Grade 2	Grade 3	Grade 4	Grade 5	Course 1	Course 2	Course 3	Pre-Algebra	Algebra 1	Geometry
Identify irrational numbers								●	●	●		●	●
Represent irrational, real numbers on a number line								●	●	●		●	●
Identify and classify real numbers								●	●	●	●	●	●
Estimate square roots								●	●	●		●	●

Scope and Sequence

Number and Operations

	PreK	Kindergarten	Grade 1	Grade 2	Grade 3	Grade 4	Grade 5	Course 1	Course 2	Course 3	Pre-Algebra	Algebra 1	Geometry
Understand Operations													
Model, meaning of addition	●	●	●	●	●	●	●						
Model, meaning of subtraction	●	●	●	●	●	●	●						
Meaning of multiplication: repeated addition, equal groups, arrays				●	●	●	●						
Meaning of division: equal groups, repeated subtraction				●	●	●	●						
Inverse operations: relate addition and subtraction; multiplication and division			●	●	●	●	●						
Check subtraction by adding				●	●	●	●						

	PreK	Kindergarten	Grade 1	Grade 2	Grade 3	Grade 4	Grade 5	Course 1	Course 2	Course 3	Pre-Algebra	Algebra 1	Geometry
Operations: Whole Numbers													
Add whole numbers — Basic facts	●	●	●	●	●	●	●	●	●	●			
Fact families		●	●	●	●	●	●	●	●	●			
Count on, doubles			●	●	●	●	●						
Number line			●	●	●	●	●	●	●				
Algorithm (regroup), partial sums			●	●	●	●	●	●	●	●			
Three or more addends				●	●	●	●	●	●	●			
Subtract whole numbers — Basic facts	●	●	●	●	●	●	●	●	●	●			
Fact families			●	●	●	●	●	●	●	●			
Count back			●	●	●	●	●	●	●	●			
Number line			●	●	●	●	●	●	●	●			
Algorithm (regroup)			●	●	●	●	●	●	●	●			

● Introduce   ● Develop   ● Reinforce   ● Maintain and Apply   ● Prerequisite Skills

	PreK	Kindergarten	Grade 1	Grade 2	Grade 3	Grade 4	Grade 5	Course 1	Course 2	Course 3	Pre-Algebra	Algebra 1	Geometry
Multiply whole numbers Basic facts				●	●	●	●	●	●				
Fact families, related facts				●	●	●	●	●	●				
Multiply three numbers					●	●	●	●	●				
Algorithm (regroup)				●	●	●	●	●	●				
Divide whole numbers Basic facts				●	●	●	●	●	●				
Fact families, related facts				●	●	●	●	●	●				
Algorithm					●	●	●	●	●				
Remainders					●	●	●	●	●				

Operations: Fractions

	PreK	Kindergarten	Grade 1	Grade 2	Grade 3	Grade 4	Grade 5	Course 1	Course 2	Course 3	Pre-Algebra	Algebra 1	Geometry
Add and subtract fractions and mixed numbers Like denominators						●	●	●	●	●	●		
Unlike denominators						●	●	●	●	●	●		
Multiply and divide fractions, mixed numbers							●	●	●	●	●		

Operations: Decimals

	PreK	Kindergarten	Grade 1	Grade 2	Grade 3	Grade 4	Grade 5	Course 1	Course 2	Course 3	Pre-Algebra	Algebra 1	Geometry
Add and subtract decimals Money amounts				●	●	●	●						
Non-money amounts						●	●	●	●	●	●	●	
Multiply decimals							●	●	●	●	●	●	
Divide decimals							●	●	●	●	●	●	

Operations: Integers, Rational, Real Numbers

	PreK	Kindergarten	Grade 1	Grade 2	Grade 3	Grade 4	Grade 5	Course 1	Course 2	Course 3	Pre-Algebra	Algebra 1	Geometry
Add and subtract integers								●	●	●	●	●	●
Multiply and divide integers								●	●	●	●	●	●

Scope and Sequence

Number and Operations

Number and Operations	PreK	Kindergarten	Grade 1	Grade 2	Grade 3	Grade 4	Grade 5	Course 1	Course 2	Course 3	Pre-Algebra	Algebra 1	Geometry
Rules of exponents								◐	●	●	●	◐	●
Add, subtract, multiply, and divide rational numbers									◐	●	●	●	●
Add, subtract, multiply, and divide real numbers												◐	●

Mental Arithmetic and Estimation Strategies

	PreK	Kindergarten	Grade 1	Grade 2	Grade 3	Grade 4	Grade 5	Course 1	Course 2	Course 3	Pre-Algebra	Algebra 1	Geometry
Add and subtract multiples of powers of 10			●	●	●	●	●	●	●				
Multiply multiples of powers of 10				◐	◐	●	●	●	●				
Divide multiples of powers of 10					◐	●	●	●	●				
Use addition properties						◐	●	●	●				
Use compensation						◐	●	●	●				
Estimation	◐	◐	●	●	●	●	●	●	●				
Rounding		●	◐	●	●	●	●	●	●				
Estimate sums		●	◐	●	◐	◐	●	●	●	●			
Estimate differences		●	◐	●	◐	◐	●	●	●	●			
Estimate products				◐	◐	●	●	●	●	●			
Estimate quotients					◐	●	●	●	●	●			
Use compatible numbers, clustering					●	●	●	●	●				
Estimate with fractions									◐	●	●		
Estimate percents								◐	●	●	◐		
Estimate square roots									◐	●	●	●	●

● Introduce   ● Develop   ● Reinforce   ● Maintain and Apply   ● Prerequisite Skills

Algebra

Use Patterns

	PreK	Kindergarten	Grade 1	Grade 2	Grade 3	Grade 4	Grade 5	Course 1	Course 2	Course 3	Pre-Algebra	Algebra 1	Geometry
Sort and classify by attribute	●	●	●	●	●								
Identify, describe patterns	●	●	●	●	●	●	●						
Extend patterns	●	●	●	●	●	●	●						
Create patterns	●	●	●	●	●	●	●						
Number patterns			●	●	●	●	●						
Use addition and subtraction patterns				●	●	●	●						
Use multiplication patterns					●	●	●						
Use division patterns							●						

Properties

	PreK	Kindergarten	Grade 1	Grade 2	Grade 3	Grade 4	Grade 5	Course 1	Course 2	Course 3	Pre-Algebra	Algebra 1	Geometry
Associative and Commutative Properties			●	●	●	●	●	●	●	●	●	●	●
Identity Properties			●	●	●	●	●	●	●	●	●	●	●
Zero Property of Multiplication				●	●	●	●	●	●	●	●	●	●
Distributive Property					●	●	●	●	●	●	●	●	●
Order of operations					●	●	●	●	●	●	●	●	●
Addition and Subtraction Properties of Equality								●	●	●	●	●	●
Multiplication and Division Properties of Equality								●	●	●	●	●	●
Additive Inverse Property								●	●	●	●	●	●
Multiplicative Inverse Property									●	●	●	●	●
Closure Property												●	●
Properties of equalities and inequalities												●	●

Scope and Sequence

Algebra

Algebraic Representations

	PreK	Kindergarten	Grade 1	Grade 2	Grade 3	Grade 4	Grade 5	Course 1	Course 2	Course 3	Pre-Algebra	Algebra 1	Geometry
Write and solve number sentences using symbols, +, −, =		●	●	●	●	●	●						
Missing addends or factors			●	●	●	●	●						
Variables, expressions, equations				●	●	●	●	●	●	●	●	●	●
Order of operations					●	●	●	●	●	●	●	●	●
Evaluate algebraic expressions					●	●	●	●	●	●	●	●	●
Write algebraic expressions and equations				●	●	●	●	●	●	●	●	●	●
Use formulas					●	●	●	●	●	●	●	●	●
Inequalities with variables									●	●	●	●	
Equivalent expressions; simplify expressions								●	●	●	●	●	●
Monomials									●	●		●	●
Operations with monomials									●	●		●	●
Polynomials, definition											●	●	●
Operations with polynomials											●	●	●
Factor polynomials												●	●
Pythagorean Theorem								●	●	●	●	●	●
Distance formula									●	●	●	●	●
Radical expressions												●	●
Rational expressions, algebraic fractions											●	●	●

● Introduce   ● Develop   ● Reinforce   ● Maintain and Apply   ● Prerequisite Skills

Solve Equations and Inequalities

	PreK	Kindergarten	Grade 1	Grade 2	Grade 3	Grade 4	Grade 5	Course 1	Course 2	Course 3	Pre-Algebra	Algebra 1	Geometry
Addition and subtraction equations					●	◐	●	●	●	●	●	●	
Multiplication and division equations						◐	●	●	●	●	●	●	
Multiple-step equations								◐	●	●	●	●	
Equations with variables on both sides									◐	●	●	●	
Solve inequalities									●	◐	●	●	
Graph inequalities									◐	●	●	●	
Multiple-step inequalities										◐	●	●	
Compound inequalities											◐	●	
Absolute-value equations, inequalities											◐		
Quadratic equations, graphing and factoring											◐		

Graph Linear and Nonlinear Equations and Inequalities

	PreK	Kindergarten	Grade 1	Grade 2	Grade 3	Grade 4	Grade 5	Course 1	Course 2	Course 3	Pre-Algebra	Algebra 1	Geometry
Relationships between equations and their graphs						●	●	◐	●	●	●	●	
Linear equations								◐	●	●	●	●	
Rate of change								◐	◐	●	●	●	
Slope								◐	●	●	●	●	
Intercepts								◐	●	●	●	●	
Slope-intercept form								◐	◐	●	●	●	
Point-slope form									●	◐	●	●	
Systems of linear equations and inequalities, graph and solve									◐	◐	◐	●	

Scope and Sequence

Algebra

Functions and Relations	PreK	Kindergarten	Grade 1	Grade 2	Grade 3	Grade 4	Grade 5	Course 1	Course 2	Course 3	Pre-Algebra	Algebra 1	Geometry
Function tables				●	●	●	●	●	●	●	●	●	
Function rules				●	●	●	●	●	●	●	●	●	
Definition of function				●	●	●	●	●	●	●	●	●	
Definition of relation, mapping												●	
Domain and range of functions									●	●	●	●	
f(x) notation									●			●	
Vertical-line test for functions											●	●	
Identify linear and nonlinear functions, relationships									●	●	●	●	
Graph ordered pairs					●	●	●	●	●	●	●	●	
Graph functions						●			●	●	●	●	
Graph relationships								●	●	●	●	●	
Model real-world data							●	●	●	●	●	●	
Proportional relationships, direct variation								●	●	●	●	●	
Inverse variation								●			●	●	
Quadratic functions										●	●	●	
Exponential functions											●	●	
Rational functions												●	
Absolute-value functions												●	
Families of linear functions										●	●	●	
Families of nonlinear functions										●	●	●	
Arithmetic sequences								●	●	●	●	●	

● Introduce   ● Develop   ● Reinforce   ● Maintain and Apply   ● Prerequisite Skills

Measurement

Length, Weight, Mass, Area, Capacity, Volume	PreK	Kindergarten	Grade 1	Grade 2	Grade 3	Grade 4	Grade 5	Course 1	Course 2	Course 3	Pre-Algebra	Algebra 1	Geometry
Compare and order	●	●	●	●	●	●	●						
Nonstandard units	●	●	●	●	●								
Customary units			●	●	●	●	●	●	●	●	●	●	●
Metric units				●	●	●	●	●	●	●	●	●	●
Estimate measurements				●	●	●	●						
Convert units within a system				●	●	●	●	●	●	●	●	●	●

Temperature	PreK	Kindergarten	Grade 1	Grade 2	Grade 3	Grade 4	Grade 5	Course 1	Course 2	Course 3	Pre-Algebra	Algebra 1	Geometry
Temperature (Celsius, Fahrenheit)		●	●	●	●	●	●	●	●	●	●	●	

Time	PreK	Kindergarten	Grade 1	Grade 2	Grade 3	Grade 4	Grade 5	Course 1	Course 2	Course 3	Pre-Algebra	Algebra 1	Geometry
Morning, afternoon, evening	●	●	●	●	●	●							
Calendar	●	●	●	●	●	●	●						
Tell time, digital/analog		●	●	●	●	●	●	●					
Estimate time		●	●	●	●	●	●	●					
Elapsed time				●	●	●	●	●					
Order events		●	●	●	●	●	●						
Units of time		●	●	●	●	●	●	●					

Money	PreK	Kindergarten	Grade 1	Grade 2	Grade 3	Grade 4	Grade 5	Course 1	Course 2	Course 3	Pre-Algebra	Algebra 1	Geometry
Recognize and count coins			●	●	●	●	●						
Compare money amounts			●	●	●	●	●						
Find values of coins			●	●	●	●	●						
Make change					●	●	●						
Fractions, decimals, and money					●	●	●						

Scope and Sequence

Measurement

Measurement Formulas and Techniques

Measurement	PreK	Kindergarten	Grade 1	Grade 2	Grade 3	Grade 4	Grade 5	Course 1	Course 2	Course 3	Pre-Algebra	Algebra 1	Geometry
Use formulas						●	●	●	●	●	●	●	●

Length

	PreK	Kindergarten	Grade 1	Grade 2	Grade 3	Grade 4	Grade 5	Course 1	Course 2	Course 3	Pre-Algebra	Algebra 1	Geometry
Perimeter of rectangle					●	●	●	●	●	●	●	●	●
Circumference of circle								●	●	●	●	●	●

Area and Surface Area

	PreK	Kindergarten	Grade 1	Grade 2	Grade 3	Grade 4	Grade 5	Course 1	Course 2	Course 3	Pre-Algebra	Algebra 1	Geometry
Compare and order areas	●	●	●	●	●	●							
Estimate area				●	●	●							
Area of rectangle, square				●	●	●	●	●	●	●	●	●	●
Area of parallelogram							●	●	●	●	●	●	●
Area of triangle							●	●	●	●	●	●	●
Area of trapezoid								●	●	●	●	●	●
Area of circle								●	●	●	●	●	●
Area of composite figures							●	●	●	●	●	●	●
Surface area of cube, rectangular prism							●	●	●	●	●	●	●
Surface area of cylinder								●	●	●	●	●	●
Surface area of cone, pyramid, sphere										●	●	●	●

Volume

	PreK	Kindergarten	Grade 1	Grade 2	Grade 3	Grade 4	Grade 5	Course 1	Course 2	Course 3	Pre-Algebra	Algebra 1	Geometry
Volume of cube, rectangular prism							●	●	●	●	●	●	●
Volume of cylinder								●	●	●	●	●	●
Volume of cone, pyramid, sphere										●	●	●	●
Angle measurement in degrees							●	●	●	●	●	●	●

● Introduce　● Develop　● Reinforce　● Maintain and Apply　● Prerequisite Skills

	PreK	Kindergarten	Grade 1	Grade 2	Grade 3	Grade 4	Grade 5	Course 1	Course 2	Course 3	Pre-Algebra	Algebra 1	Geometry
Precision and significant digits												●	
Indirect measurement								●	●	●	●	●	●

Geometry

Plane and Solid Shapes

	PreK	Kindergarten	Grade 1	Grade 2	Grade 3	Grade 4	Grade 5	Course 1	Course 2	Course 3	Pre-Algebra	Algebra 1	Geometry
Identify attributes of plane shapes	●	●	●	●	●	●	●	●	●	●	●	●	●
Identify attributes of solid shapes	●	●	●	●	●	●	●	●	●	●	●	●	●
Classify and describe properties of plane shapes	●	●	●	●	●	●	●	●	●	●	●	●	●
Classify and describe properties of solid shapes	●	●	●	●	●	●	●	●	●	●	●	●	●
Relate plane and solid figures	●	●	●	●	●	●	●	●	●	●	●	●	●
Lines, line segments, rays					●	●	●	●	●	●	●	●	●
Parallel, perpendicular lines					●	●	●	●	●	●	●	●	●
Classify and measure angles					●	●	●	●	●	●	●	●	●
Angle relationships								●	●	●	●	●	●
Identify and define polygons		●	●	●	●	●	●	●	●	●	●	●	●
Classify quadrilaterals					●	●	●	●	●	●	●	●	●
Classify triangles					●	●	●	●	●	●	●	●	●
Sum of angles in a triangle								●	●	●	●	●	●
Sum of angles of polygons								●	●	●	●	●	●

Scope and Sequence

Geometry

Geometry	PreK	Kindergarten	Grade 1	Grade 2	Grade 3	Grade 4	Grade 5	Course 1	Course 2	Course 3	Pre-Algebra	Algebra 1	Geometry
Parts of circles							●	●	●	●	●	●	●
Congruent figures				●	◐	●	●	●	●	●	●	●	●
Similar figures								◐	●	●	●	●	●
Corresponding parts								◐	●	●	●	●	●
Scale drawings									◐	●	●	●	●
Right triangles and parts									◐	●	●	●	●
Pythagorean Theorem									◐	●	●	●	●
Right triangle trigonometry													◐

Coordinate Geometry

Coordinate Geometry	PreK	Kindergarten	Grade 1	Grade 2	Grade 3	Grade 4	Grade 5	Course 1	Course 2	Course 3	Pre-Algebra	Algebra 1	Geometry
Position and direction	●	◐	●	●	●	●	●						
Graph ordered pairs				●	◐	●	●	●	●	●	●	●	●
Horizontal, vertical distance on a grid			●	◐	●	●	●	●	●	●	●	●	●
Distance formula											◐	●	●
Graph linear equations								◐	●	●	●	●	●
Slope								◐	●	●	●	●	●
Slope-intercept form of line								◐	●	●	●	●	◐
Point-slope form of line												◐	●
Slope of parallel, perpendicular lines												◐	●

Transformations and Symmetry

Transformations and Symmetry	PreK	Kindergarten	Grade 1	Grade 2	Grade 3	Grade 4	Grade 5	Course 1	Course 2	Course 3	Pre-Algebra	Algebra 1	Geometry
Translations (slide)							◐	●	●	●	●	●	●
Reflections (flip)							◐	●	●	●	●	●	●

● Introduce ● Develop ● Reinforce ● Maintain and Apply ● Prerequisite Skills

	PreK	Kindergarten	Grade 1	Grade 2	Grade 3	Grade 4	Grade 5	Course 1	Course 2	Course 3	Pre-Algebra	Algebra 1	Geometry
Rotations (turn)					◐	●	●			●	●	●	●
Dilations										◐	◐	●	●
Transformations on coordinate plane						◐	◐	●	●	●	●	●	●
Symmetry (line and rotation)					●	◐	●		●	●	●	●	●
Tessellations						◐	●		●	●	●	●	●

Spatial Reasoning

	PreK	Kindergarten	Grade 1	Grade 2	Grade 3	Grade 4	Grade 5	Course 1	Course 2	Course 3	Pre-Algebra	Algebra 1	Geometry
Draw angles, lines, polygons					●	◐	●	●	◐	●			●
Constructions											◐	●	●
Draw 3-dimensional objects									◐	◐	●		●
Nets					●	●	●	●	●	●	●		◑

Data Analysis

Sort, Classify

	PreK	Kindergarten	Grade 1	Grade 2	Grade 3	Grade 4	Grade 5	Course 1	Course 2	Course 3	Pre-Algebra	Algebra 1	Geometry
Sort and classify by attribute	●	◐	●	●	●								
Use Venn diagrams		●	◐	●	●	●	●	●	●	●	●	●	●

Collect, Organize, and Display Data

	PreK	Kindergarten	Grade 1	Grade 2	Grade 3	Grade 4	Grade 5	Course 1	Course 2	Course 3	Pre-Algebra	Algebra 1	Geometry
Collect data	●	●	●	◐	●	●	●	●	●	●	◐	●	◐
Organize data with a table			●	◐	●	●	●	●	●	●	●	●	
Organize data with a graph	●	●	●	◐	●	●	●	●	◐	●	◐	●	
Frequency tables; tally charts			●	◐	●	●	●	●	●	●	●	●	●

Scope and Sequence

Data Analysis

Data Analysis	PreK	Kindergarten	Grade 1	Grade 2	Grade 3	Grade 4	Grade 5	Course 1	Course 2	Course 3	Pre-Algebra	Algebra 1	Geometry
Surveys		●	●	◐	◐	●	●	●	●	●	●	●	
Samples								●	●	●	●	●	
Random samples								●	◐	●	●	●	
Use sampling to predict								●	◐	●	●	●	

Represent Data

Represent Data	PreK	Kindergarten	Grade 1	Grade 2	Grade 3	Grade 4	Grade 5	Course 1	Course 2	Course 3	Pre-Algebra	Algebra 1	Geometry
Real graphs	●	◐											
Picture graphs, pictograph	●	◐	●	●	●	●	●						
Bar graphs; double bar graphs		●	◐	●	●	●	●	●	●	●	●	●	
Line plots				◐	●	●	●	●	●	●	●	●	
Circle graphs								◐	●	●	●	●	●
Line graphs							◐	●	●	●	●	●	
Stem-and-leaf plots								◐	●	●	●	●	
Box-and-whisker plots									◐	●	●	●	
Histograms								◐	●	●	●		
Scatter plots								◐	●	◐	●		
Fitted lines on scatter plots								◐	◐	●	●		
Choose an appropriate graph/display							◐	●	●	●	●	●	

Make Inferences and Predictions

Make Inferences and Predictions	PreK	Kindergarten	Grade 1	Grade 2	Grade 3	Grade 4	Grade 5	Course 1	Course 2	Course 3	Pre-Algebra	Algebra 1	Geometry
Use data		●	◐	●	●	●	●	●	●	●	●	●	
Mode		●	●	●	●	●	●	●	●	●	●	●	
Median						◐	●	●	◐	●	●	●	
Mean								◐	●	●	◐	●	

● Introduce ● Develop ● Reinforce ● Maintain and Apply ● Prerequisite Skills

	PreK	Kindergarten	Grade 1	Grade 2	Grade 3	Grade 4	Grade 5	Course 1	Course 2	Course 3	Pre-Algebra	Algebra 1	Geometry
Range						●	●	●	●	●	●		
Outliers					●	●	●	●	●	●	●	●	
Quartiles									●	●		●	
Misleading graphs and statistics									●	●	●	●	
Make predictions from graphs						●	●	●	●	●	●	●	
Make predictions from a sample								●	●	●	●	●	

Probability

	PreK	Kindergarten	Grade 1	Grade 2	Grade 3	Grade 4	Grade 5	Course 1	Course 2	Course 3	Pre-Algebra	Algebra 1	Geometry
Certain, probable, impossible		●	●	●	●	●	●						
Likely and unlikely, compare likelihoods			●	●	●	●	●						
Predict outcomes					●	●	●	●	●	●	●	●	
Outcomes and sample space						●	●	●	●	●	●	●	
Probability of a simple event						●	●	●	●	●	●	●	
Complementary events								●	●	●	●	●	
Composite events: independent, dependent									●	●	●	●	
Mutually exclusive or inclusive events, disjoint											●	●	
Experimental probability						●	●	●	●	●	●	●	
Theoretical probability						●	●	●	●	●	●	●	
Probability and ratio								●	●	●	●	●	
Simulations									●	●	●	●	
Tree diagrams						●	●	●	●	●	●	●	
Fundamental Counting Principle							●	●	●	●	●	●	

Scope and Sequence

Data Analysis

	PreK	Kindergarten	Grade 1	Grade 2	Grade 3	Grade 4	Grade 5	Course 1	Course 2	Course 3	Pre-Algebra	Algebra 1	Geometry
Combinations						●	●	◑	●	●	●		
Permutations								◑	●	●	●		
Probability distributions												◑	

Problem Solving

Strategies and Skills

	PreK	Kindergarten	Grade 1	Grade 2	Grade 3	Grade 4	Grade 5	Course 1	Course 2	Course 3	Pre-Algebra	Algebra 1	Geometry
Look for a pattern	●	◑	◑	●	●	●	●	●	●	●	●	●	●
Act it out, use objects, use simulation		●	◑	●	●	●	●	●	●	●	●	●	●
Guess and check		●	●	◑	●	●	●	●	●	●	●	●	●
Draw a picture or diagram		●	◑	●	●	●	●	●	●	●	●	●	●
Make a table		●	●	●	●	●	●	●	●	●	●	●	●
Make a graph		●	●	●	◑	●	●	●	●	●	●	●	●
Make a list			◑	◑	●	●	●	●	●	●	●	●	●
Make a model	●		◑	●	●	●	●	●	●	●	●	●	●
Work backward			●	◑	●	●	●	●	●	●	●	●	●
Use logical reasoning		●	◑	◑	●	●	●	●	●	●	●	◑	●
Use a four-step plan		●	◑	●	●	●	●	●	●	●	●	●	●
Choose a strategy			◑	◑	●	●	●	●	●	●	●	●	●
Choose an operation				●	●	●	●	●	●	●	●	●	●
Check for reasonableness		●	●	◑	●	●	●	●	●	●	●	●	●

● Introduce   ● Develop   ● Reinforce   ● Maintain and Apply   ● Prerequisite Skills

	PreK	Kindergarten	Grade 1	Grade 2	Grade 3	Grade 4	Grade 5	Course 1	Course 2	Course 3	Pre-Algebra	Algebra 1	Geometry
Write a number sentence			●	◐	●	●	●						
Write an equation						◐	●	●	●	●	●	●	●
Use formulas					●	●	●	●	●	●	●	◐	●
Decide whether to estimate or compute					◐	●	●	●	●	●	●	●	●
Identify missing or extra information					◐	●	●						
Solve multi-step problems						◐	●	●	●	●	●	●	●
Conduct a poll or survey			●	◐	●	●	●	●	●	●	●	●	
Solve a simpler problem					◐	●	●	●	●	●	●	●	●

Mathematical Reasoning and Justification

	PreK	Kindergarten	Grade 1	Grade 2	Grade 3	Grade 4	Grade 5	Course 1	Course 2	Course 3	Pre-Algebra	Algebra 1	Geometry
Use mathematical reasoning		●	◐	●	●	●	●	●	●	●	◐	◐	◐
Use Venn diagrams		●	◐	●	●	●	●	●	●	●	●	●	●
Explain, justify, and defend reasoning			●	◐	●	●	●	●	●	●	●	◐	◐
Check validity of calculated results			●	◐	●	●	●	●	●	●	●	●	●
Create problems					◐	●	●	●	●	●	●	●	●
Write informal mathematical arguments				●	◐	●	●	●	●	●	●	●	●
Make and test conjectures, counterexamples						●	●	◐	◐	◐	●	●	●
Inductive reasoning								◐	●	●	●	●	●
Deductive reasoning								◐	●	●	●	●	●
Develop a proof: paragraph, algebraic, coordinate, indirect												◐	●

Reading Strategies

How Can I Help My Students Read and Understand the Textbook?

Professional Development

Mathematics teachers do not have to be reading teachers to help students read and understand their textbooks. Often poor readers lack interest in the topic, have trouble concentrating, cannot understand a word or sentence, or are confused as to how the information fits together.

Activate Prior Knowledge

Activating prior knowledge provides opportunities for students to discover and articulate what they already know about key concepts and ideas. It stimulates student interest and prepares students to incorporate new information into a larger picture. In addition, it helps the teacher to determine a starting place for instruction.

✔ Write the topic on the board and have students brainstorm what they know about it. Record their responses on the board.

✔ Ask general or specific questions about the topic and see how students respond to them.

"The research evidence on adolescents and their learning indicates that students must learn how to take notes, use graphic organizers, focus on vocabulary, and develop their thinking through writing. In other words, students must read, write, speak, listen, and view content in order to learn."

Douglas Fisher, Ph.D.
San Diego State University
Reading Consultant

✔ Use the Anticipation Guide from the *Chapter Resource Masters*. It provides a series of statements about the concepts in the chapter. Students read each statement and tell whether they agree or disagree, based on their prior understandings and experiences.

✔ Use a K-W-L-H or K-W-L chart to activate prior knowledge and set reading purposes. Students identify what they already **know** (or think they know) and what they **want** to find out about the topic. After reading, students complete the chart.

K	W	L	H
What I **Know**	What I **Want** to Find Out	What I **Learned**	**How** I Can Learn More

Set Reading Purposes

Reading is a purposeful activity. We read to find answers to specific questions, to satisfy curiosity, and to be entertained.

✔ Have students preview the lesson. Tell students to read the title, bolded words, and key concept boxes. Draw students' attention to diagrams, tables, and other visuals and their captions. Discuss how these will help comprehension.

✔ Prompt students to predict what they might learn in the lesson, based on their preview. Invite them to list additional questions they hope to answer studying the lesson. Have them identify possible problems, such as unfamiliar words or ideas.

✔ Discuss the need to "shift gears" to a lower reading speed when reading. Support students as they plan how best to read a lesson—slowly, to watch for new vocabulary and ideas, or quickly, to review previously learned ideas. They can also discuss new information with a buddy as they read.

Vocabulary Development

Vocabulary knowledge and reading comprehension are closely related.

✔ Before students read, preteach vocabulary that is crucial for understanding key topics and concepts.

✔ Relate new vocabulary to known words and ideas.

✔ If a student encounters an unfamiliar word while reading, have him or her try to pronounce it aloud. Sometimes saying the word will trigger one's memory of its meaning.

✔ Encourage students to use the context of surrounding words, sentences, and diagrams to determine a word's meaning.

✔ If context clues and structural analysis fail to help a student understand an important word as they read, have students find the definition in a glossary or dictionary. If the word is not critical for understanding, have students note the word and read on. Later, have students reread the word in context. If the meaning is still unclear, have students consult the dictionary.

Taking Notes

Taking notes challenges readers to determine what is most important and to organize information in a way that makes sense. Note-taking can also help students stay focused as they read. Reviewing notes can build students' retention of important information.

✔ Have students take notes after they have read each paragraph or example rather than the entire lesson. This helps them focus on important ideas and details and prevents them from losing track of the flow of information.
✔ Remind students to look for graphic elements that highlight important items. These include colored text, boxed text, and large or bold fonts.
✔ Have students take notes using note cards. Notes should be recorded in the students' own words and labeled with the page number where the entire text appears. They can also use their Foldables™ for that chapter or their Noteables™ Interactive Study Notebook.
✔ To use notes to review a lesson, have students read through the notes, highlighting the most important information. As they review, encourage students to annotate their notes, making

connections between related ideas and clarifying difficult concepts.

Summarizing

Summarizing demands that students identify the most important ideas and details to create a streamlined version of the text.

✔ After reading the section, have students recall as much of the information as possible. If the main idea and its supporting details are presented in a certain order, make sure

students can recall that organization.
✔ As they summarize, students should try to answer the following questions:
• How do the examples and key words fit into the main idea?
• How does the lesson relate to the concepts studied earlier?

STUDY SKILL

Project CRISS [**CR**eating **I**ndependence through **S**tudent-owned **S**trategies] is a research-based staff development program created to help students better organize, understand and retain course information. In short, students receiving the CRISS method of instruction will "LEARN HOW TO LEARN."

CRISS strategies are designed to develop thoughtful and independent readers and learners.

To enhance student learning, CRISS employs several concepts drawn from cognitive psychology.

• Students must be able to integrate new information with prior knowledge.
• Students need to be actively involved in their own learning by discussing, writing, and organizing information.
• Students must self-monitor to identify which strategies are the most effective for their own learning.

These behaviors need to be taught by content teachers to maximize student learning.

For more information on Project CRISS℠, visit www.projectcriss.com.

Cooperative Group Strategies

How Can I Use Cooperative Learning to Teach Mathematics?

Today's social and economic climate requires flexibility. Workers must be able to function independently, work well with groups, and engage in fair-minded competition. For this reason, most educators recommend a healthy balance of instructional strategies to foster cooperative, competitive, and individualistic styles of problem solving and learning. Cooperative learning requires students to work together—each with a specific task—to pursue a common goal. Because part of each student's evaluation is determined by the overall quality of the group's work, students help one another accomplish the group goal.

How Do I Form Cooperative Groups?

✔ **Composition** Most experts recommend that cooperative groups be heterogeneous, reflecting a range of student abilities, backgrounds, and learning styles. However, this does not necessarily mean that students should be assigned to groups on a random basis.

✔ **Group Size** The size of cooperative groups can change, depending upon the task. Some cooperative tasks are best accomplished in pairs. For most projects, groups of three to five students are ideal.

✔ **Abilities** Consider the tasks and projects the groups will undertake as you make group assignments. You may want to make sure each group has a strong manager, a strong writer, a strong artist, a good listener, and so forth.

✔ **Balance** Some teachers use a "family-of-five" approach to grouping. A strong leader heads each group. Two pairs of students with opposing styles or strengths complete the "family." Paired students might exhibit traits such as outgoing and shy, creative and conventional, spontaneous and methodical, and so on. Each group continues to work together throughout the semester or year, with the goal that students develop greater flexibility in their own problem-solving abilities and greater respect for the contributions of others.

✔ **Roles** In most instances, you will want to assign a specific role for each student to play in a group, such as designer, moderator, recorder, researcher, presenter, graphic artist, actor, and so forth. Roles should be interdependent, requiring students to rely upon one another in order to successfully carry out their individual responsibilities. As students gain experience in working in cooperative groups, turn over more of the responsibility for establishing individual roles and responsibilities to the group.

How Do I Help Groups Run Smoothly?

✔ **Seating Arrangements** Explain how and where groups should sit. Pairs can sit with desks or chairs face-to-face. Larger groups do well with desks or chairs gathered in a circle or with students seated around a table.

✔ **Warm-Ups** Provide an introductory activity for new groups. Even when students know one another, they can benefit by making formal introductions and sharing their thoughts on a sentence starter, such as "If I could go anywhere in the world, I would go to . . ." or "If I could have lived at any period in history, I would choose. . ."

✔ **Rules** Set clear expectations and rules for groups. Typical rules include addressing group members by name, making eye contact, listening politely, expressing disagreement with respect, welcoming others' questions, valuing others' contributions, providing positive feedback, and assisting others when asked.

How Do I Use Cooperative Groups in My Classroom?

✔ **Share and Tell** Have students form groups of four. Assign each group member a number between one and four. Ask a factual recall question. Have group members discuss the question and come up with an answer. Call out a number between one and four. The student with that number who is first to raise his or her hand answers the question. The group earns a point for a correct answer.

✔ **Circle Partners** Have the class separate into two equal groups and form two circles, with one circle inside the other. Each student faces a partner in the opposing circle. Ask a question and have partners discuss the answer. If partners do not know the answer they can ask another pair for help. Then, call on students in the inside circle, the outside circle, or all students to say the answer aloud together.

✔ **In the Know** Provide students with a set of end-of-chapter questions or other questions covering content you want students to master. Tell students to circulate around the room to find someone who can answer a question on the worksheet. After listening to the answer, the student paraphrases it, writes the answer on the worksheet, and asks the "expert" to read and sign off on the answer if it is correct. Students move on to find a student to answer the next question. The process continues until students have completed their worksheets.

✔ **Open-Ended Projects** The best long-term projects for cooperative groups are those that are open-ended and multidimensional. That is, the task or question should have many possible answers and should lend itself to many different presentation possibilities.

Multiple intelligences Appropriate projects should challenge students and allow students of various abilities and backgrounds to contribute significantly to solving the problem and executing the project. One way to assess the validity of a potential project is to see whether it requires the use of many different strengths or "intelligences."

Assigning roles Because of the complexity of long-term projects, it is essential that students have clearly assigned roles and responsibilities. Once cooperative groups are established and successful in your classroom, be sure to vary the assignments given to each student from project to project.

✔ **Deadlines** Define interim and final deadlines to encourage students to pace their efforts appropriately.

How Do I Assess Group and Individual Efforts?

✔ **Expectations** As with any assignment, set clear guidelines and high expectations for projects. Show models of excellent past projects, if possible, and define what criteria projects must meet to earn the highest grade.

✔ **Group and Individual Grades** Before students begin, define what percentage of the grade will be based on group work and how much will be based on individual effort. Many teachers give two equally weighted grades: a group grade—the same for each team member—and an individual grade.

✔ **Self-Assessment** Provide a checklist or rating scale for each group member. Have students evaluate their own contribution to the group, as well as the contributions of other group members. In addition to assessing the quality of the finished product, have students evaluate the processes they used within the group, such as showing respect for others' ideas. Provide space on the evaluation sheet for students to explain why they rated themselves and group members as they did.

Troubleshooting

Advice from Carey Boswell, M.Ed.
Humble Independent School District
Humble, Texas

Modern research overwhelmingly suggests that student learning is enhanced when cooperative groups are used in the classroom. Like many other teachers, I was uncertain of how much learning was taking place when I set up cooperative groups. I struggled with noise and control issues and off-task behavior by some students. I found a solution, though.

A cooperative group activity occurs whenever a student works with another student. Cooperative groups do not have to be large groups. Smaller groups ensure that all students are engaged and contribute to the group effort. Smaller groups also guarantee that members perform multiple tasks so that real learning occurs. I often combine two or more small groups into a larger group for short comparative tasks. After making this small adjustment, I am able to assign cooperative group tasks to students at least once a week and student performance, comprehension, and learning has increased in my classroom.

Differentiated Instruction

How Can I Help ALL My Students Learn Mathematics?

Professional Development

"To differentiate instruction, teachers must acknowledge students differences in background knowledge, current English language skills, learning styles and preferences, interests, needs, and react accordingly. Some of the general guidelines for differentiating instruction include:
- Link assessment with instruction.
- Clarify key concepts and generalizations.
- Emphasize critical and creative thinking.
- Include teacher- and student-selected tasks."

Nancy Frey, Ph.D.
San Diego State University
Differentiated Instruction Consultant

Today's classroom contains students from a variety of backgrounds and with a variety of learning styles, strengths, and challenges. With careful planning, you can address the needs of all students in the social studies classroom. The following tips for instruction can assist your efforts to help all students reach their maximum potential.

✔ Survey students to discover their individual differences. Use interest inventories of their unique talents so you can encourage contributions in the classroom.
✔ Model respect of others. Adolescents crave social acceptance. Your behavior will set the tone for how students treat one another.
✔ Expand opportunities for success. Provide a variety of instructional activities that reinforce skills and concepts.
✔ Establish measurable objectives and decide how you can best help students meet them.
✔ Celebrate successes and praise "work in progress."
✔ Keep it simple. Avoid

overwhelming students with too many goals at one time.
✔ Assign cooperative group projects that challenge all students to contribute to solving a problem or creating a product.

Students with Learning Disabilities

✔ Provide support and structure. Clearly specify rules, assignments, and responsibilities.
✔ Practice skills frequently. Use games and drills to help maintain student interest.
✔ Incorporate many modalities into the learning process. Provide opportunities to say, hear, write, read, and act out important concepts and information.
✔ Link new skills and concepts to those already mastered.
✔ Allow students to record answers on audiotape.
✔ Allow extra time to complete tests and assignments.
✔ Let students demonstrate proficiency with alternative presentations, including oral reports, role plays, art projects, and with music.

✔ Provide outlines, notes, or tape recordings of lecture material.
✔ Pair students with peer helpers, and provide class time for pair interaction.

English Language Learners

✔ Remember, students' ability to speak English does not reflect their academic abilities.
✔ Try to incorporate the students' cultural experience into your instruction. The help of a bilingual aide may be effective.
✔ Avoid cultural stereotypes.
✔ Pre-teach important vocabulary and concepts.
✔ Encourage students to preview text before they begin reading, noting headings, graphic organizers, photographs, and maps.

"English Language Learners need teachers who understand the current and historic mathematical functions of their students' originating countries and cultures, make mathematics meaningful by tying instruction to local languages and cultures, and are curious and fascinated themselves about mathematics."

Mary A. Avalos, Ph.D.
University of Miami
English Language Learner Consultant

Gifted Students

"Instruction for mathematically gifted children should help the student:

• Understand and appreciate mathematics and its place in the world.

• Learn to think deeply and with insight.

• Take intellectual risks.

• Have confidence in their ability to solve difficult problems independently.

• Understand and value their gift."

Ed Zaccaro
Bellevue, Iowa
Gifted and Talented
Consultant

Students with Physical Challenges

✔ Openly discuss with the student any uncertainties you have about when to offer aid.

✔ Ask parents or therapists and students what special devices or procedures are needed, and whether any special safety precautions need to be taken.

✔ Welcome students with physical challenges into all activities, including field trips, special events, and projects.

Visual Impairments

✔ Facilitate independence. Modify assignments as needed.

✔ Teach classmates how and when to serve as guides.

✔ Limit unnecessary noise in the classroom, if it distracts the student with visual impairments.

✔ Provide tactile models whenever possible.

✔ Foster a spirit of inclusion.

✔ Team the student with a sighted peer for written work.

Students with Hearing Impairments

✔ Seat students where they can see your lip movements easily and where they can avoid visual distractions.

✔ Avoid standing with your back to the window or light source.

✔ Use an overhead projector to maintain eye contact while writing.

✔ Seat students where they can see speakers.

✔ Write all assignments on the board, or hand out written instructions.

✔ If the student has a manual interpreter, allow both student and interpreter to select the most favorable seating arrangements.

✔ Teach students to look directly at each other when they speak.

Good Teaching Practices

✔ Differentiated Instruction is simply the implementation of good teaching practices from which all students can benefit.

"Effective instruction for English language learners, called sheltered instruction, builds upon practices common in math teaching such as providing a visual representation of math problems, modeling how to solve problems and encouraging repetition and practice for mastery of skills. These students also require additional support to make instruction understandable for them since they are learning new concepts and material in a new language."

Jana Echevarria
California Statue University,
Long Beach
English Language Learner
Consultant

English Learners

What Are the Best Practices for Effective Instruction?

Anecdotal information from classroom teachers as well as evidence from research has demonstrated that the trend toward using more language in mathematics has seriously affected the achievement of students whose first language is not English. In response to this, the National Council of Teachers of Mathematics (NCTM) emphasizes communication "as an essential part of mathematics and mathematics education" and that "second-language learners in particular need to have opportunities and be given encouragement and support for speaking, writing, reading and listening in mathematics classes." Such efforts have the potential to help second-language learners overcome barriers that will facilitate "communicating to learn mathematics and learning to communicate mathematically" (NCTM, 2000).

Research done on effective mathematics instruction for English Learners (ELs) has identified the following best practices. These can be categorized as cultural, instructional, and linguistic.

Cultural Considerations

Be aware of how children's home cultures and previous experiences can contribute to their mathematics learning (Gonzalez, et al., 1995; Tikunoff, 1985). ELs bring rich, although often different, experiences with them into the classroom. Consult with bilingual staff and other cultural brokers to find out what

those experiences may be. Then use your students' prior knowledge to create contexts for instruction that are meaningful to them (Garrison & Mora, 1999). This is especially important when students are asked to solve word problems, for in order to do so, they need to be able to picture and understand the situation. This is extremely difficult to do if their experiences do not allow them to visualize what the problem is about.

" ELs bring rich, although often different, experiences with them into the classroom. Consult with bilingual staff and other cultural brokers to find out what those experiences may be. "

Instructional Considerations

Teaching the concept before the math can help ELs conceptualize what they are learning without having to master the language first (Khisty & Viego, 1999). This

can be through the use of pictures, video, manipulatives, realia (actual objects instead of just pictures or models), games, and graphic organizers (Krashen, 1981; Garrison & Mora, 1999). In addition to using these kinesthetic and visual/spatial approaches to teaching concepts, it is important to also encourage students to learn from each other. Working out problems with the aid of peers instead of individually supports the learning styles of many students who come from cultures in which collaborative learning is the norm rather than the exception.

Linguistic Considerations

If teachers structure classroom activities so that students have to speak and write about mathematics, there will be multiple opportunities to use the language of mathematics (Gee, 1992). This is best done if the teacher engages students in instructional conversations that include the use of questions (Khisty & Viego, 1999),

Vocabulary Word	Common Meaning	Mathematical Meaning
table	piece of furniture often used for eating	visual representation of data
foot	appendage at the end of one's leg	standard unit of measurement equal to 12 inches
problem	situation that is difficult to resolve	Math exercise

collaboration, and group work (Garrison & Mora, 1999). It is also important that while talking about mathematics students be encouraged to use the technical language associated with it once the concept is learned – for example, using "minus" instead of "take away" and including terms such as quotient, dividend, and divisor.

Other vocabulary that needs to be explicitly addressed are terms that can have both mathematical and common meanings. A table can be a piece of furniture, but in mathematics it often refers to a visual representation of data. Round, square, foot, and problem are other examples of such terms. As you are planning lessons, note these words and make sure that ELs understand that the common meaning is different than the technical.

In addition to vocabulary there are numerous other language features that can be problematic for ELs in the mathematics classroom. Seek out the language experts at your school, bilingual teachers and aides and teachers of English as a second language, to collaborate about how these challenges can be addressed.

Unique Needs

In order to ensure that all students achieve to their potential, Reaching All Learners stresses that teachers address the unique needs of each student in the classroom in a way that capitalizes on their strengths to meet educational goals. Best practices, such as those given above, and reasonable accommodations need to be made to promote access and achievement in mathematics for all students (Mathematics Framework for California Public Schools, 2006).

References:

California State Board of Education. (2006). *Mathematics Framework for California Public Schools.* Sacramento, CA: California State Board of Education.

Garrison, L & Mora, J. K. (1999). Adapting mathematics instruction for English language learners: The language-concept connection. In *National Council of Teachers of Mathematics. Changing the faces of mathematics: Perspectives on Latinos* (pp. 35-47). Reston VA: National Council of Teachers of Mathematics.

Gee, J. P. (1992). *The social mind, language, ideology, and social practice.* New York: Bergin & Garvey.

Gonzales, N., et al. (1995). Funds of knowledge for teaching in Latino households. *Urban Education*, 29(4) 443-470.

Khisty, L. L. & Viego, G. (1999). Challenging conventional wisdom: A case study. In *National Council of Teachers of Mathematics. Changing the faces of mathematics: Perspectives on Latinos* (pp. 35–47). Reston VA: National Council of Teachers of Mathematics.

Krashen, S. (1981). *Second language acquisition and second language learning.* London: Pergamon Press.

National Council of Teachers of Mathematics (NCTM). (2000). *Principles and standards for school mathematics.* Reston: VA: National Council of Teachers of Mathematics. 60.

Tikunoff, W. (1985). Applying significant bilingual instructional features in the classroom. Part C Bilingual Education Research Series. Rosslyn, VA: National Clearinghouse for Bilingual Education. (ERIC Document Reproduction Service No. ED 338 106).

Kathryn Heinze teaches in the Graduate School of Education at Hamline University in St. Paul, Minnesota. Since receiving an M.A. in ESL from the University of Minnesota, she has spent thirty years in the classroom as an ESL teacher and teacher educator. Recently, she has focused on helping teachers make mathematics instruction more accessible to ELs.

Professional Development

Data-Driven Decision Making

How Can I Use Assessment to Inform Instruction and Improve Student Achievement?

As mathematics educators, we understand the importance of assessment to the mathematics teaching/learning process. Assessment is an important and essential tool for teachers to use to improve instruction. In fact, it is assessment that truly distinguishes between teaching and learning. But what is it that distinguishes effective assessment from routine, calendar-based assessment? How does a teacher ensure that assessment informs teaching in a meaningful way, one that consistently shapes students learning?

Put simply, it requires data-driven decision making based on an ongoing assessment cycle. Teachers need to take the data collected from their students' performance on various assessments and use this data to make decisions on next steps for instruction.

The Assessment Cycle

To be truly effective, assessment must be embedded in the teaching and learning process, not just administered out of context at set intervals during the school year. Ongoing assessment helps teachers fine-tune the teaching process to ensure student understanding of mathematical concepts. Assessment must gather a bounty of information in order to help teachers measure student progress and glean students' potential. To this end, teachers should strive to keep accurate and dated information on their

students' progress in mathematics throughout the learning process.

Consider the following three stages of the assessment cycle:

- **Stage 1:** Identify what is to be taught, how it will be taught, and how to assess student learning.
- **Stage 2:** Gather evidence of student learning, interpret student responses, and record data.
- **Stage 3:** Act on the results. How does the data impact my teaching methods? What concepts need to be retaught?

The implementation of these types of assessments across all grade levels will help guide instruction and also provide a road map that leads students to mastery of core curriculum concepts and skills.

Assessment	
Stage 1	Do students possess crucial prerequisite skills and knowledge? Do students already know some of the material that is to be taught?
Stage 2	Are students progressing adequately toward achieving the standards?
Stage 3	Have students achieved the goals defined by a given standard of a group of standards?

Forms of Assessment

In order to effectively measure mathematical learning, teachers must make sure we include various forms of assessment. A complete assessment program should include multiple measures:

Diagnostic: The purpose of a diagnostic assessment is to determine whether the student has the skills and knowledge necessary to begin the chapter, or if the student needs intervention prior to beginning the chapter.

Formative: Daily formative assessment should include scaffolding questions as well as talking, thinking, and writing about mathematics.

Summative: Summative assessment helps the teacher determine whether the students have learned the material that they were taught throughout the chapter.

Assessment to Guide Instruction

Assessment allows the teacher to consider the strengths and challenges of students; the effectiveness of the mathematics curriculum; and the next steps that should be taken in the instructional process. Some ways to use assessment to guide instruction are:

✔ Pose a "Talk About It" question during a lesson. Encourage students to work in small groups, discussing possible solutions to the question.
✔ Probe for prior knowledge before the introduction of a new concept.
✔ Observe students while they are working either in groups or individually which will give you information regarding their understanding of mathematics.
✔ Conduct student interviews which will offer an opportunity to use questioning strategies to explore an individual student's understanding of a concept.

Assessment: A Complete System

Assessment comes in many forms: diagnostic, formative, and summative. True assessment is dynamic and rich with information concerning student potential and performance. Assessment is the contributing force in improving the teaching and learning of mathematics for all students.

It is the most effective way to distinguish between teaching and learning, both in the classroom and at the district or state level.

References:

Long, Donna. *Using Test Results to Inform Instruction and Improve Student Achievement,* Eisenhower National Clearinghouse, January 2003.

Love, Deborah. *Using Data/Getting Results: A Practical Guide for School Improvement in Mathematics and Science,* Christopher-Gordon Publishers, Inc., 2002.

National Council of Teachers of Mathematics (NCTM). *Mathematics Assessment: A Practical Handbook,* Reston, VA, 2003.

Walstrom, Deborah. *Using DATA to Improve Student Achievement,* Successline, Inc., 1999.

Entry-Level Assessment Diagnostic	Determine whether students have the skills and knowledge necessary to be successful in subsequent lessons.
Progress Monitoring Formative	Include various forms of daily assessment such as talking, thinking, and writing about mathematics.
Summative Evaluation Summative	Determine whether students have mastered the material they were taught.

Donna Long is currently the Elementary Mathematics Marketing Manager for Macmillan/McGraw-Hill. She has served as the National Mathematics Consultant for Macmillan/McGraw-Hill, the National Mathematics Assessment Consultant for CTB/McGraw-Hill, and the Mathematics/Title I Coordinator, Grades K-12, for an urban school district in Indianapolis, Indiana. She has also served as the Mathematics Program Coordinator for Curriculum and Assessment at the Indiana Department of Education.

Intervention

How Can I Bridge the Gaps in Student Learning?

It is rare to find an elementary or middle school classroom where all of the students are on the same level in mathematics. Often when standards change or students are not at the same level in mathematics, teachers feel the need to push through the mathematics curriculum, even if students are lacking prerequisite skills necessary to succeed. Teaching new mathematics standards to students is analogous to teaching students to swim: expecting students to instantly rise to the rigor of new standards, without bridging the gaps between the old and new standards, sets students up for failure.

In the opinion of many experts in the field, many mathematics programs have provided "inadequate textbooks and inadequate instruction" (Wu, 1998). To avoid such mistakes again, a successful program must provide a systematic way for teachers to bridge the mathematical gaps of students who are accustomed to less rigorous standards. For these reasons, all mathematics programs need to supply teachers with effective tools they can use for assessment and instruction of prerequisite skills.

Entry-Level Assessment: Identifying the Gaps

To accurately inform teaching decisions in the classroom, entry-level, or diagnostic, assessment should be given to students before each chapter. Entry-level assessment should not test new content; it should only test for skills required to proceed successfully into the new content. Such a test helps teachers determine what prerequisite skills students do understand and what skills need to be strengthened before proceeding into the new content. Entry-level assessment should not merely be given and then set aside; the results of entry-level assessment should be used to guide instruction throughout a chapter.

After completing this diagnostic assessment, an effective mathematics program provides different types of intervention and support for different students: intensive, strategic, benchmark, and above-level.

Intensive Intervention
This level of intervention is for students who are two or more years behind grade-level in mathematics. They need intensive instruction provided in an environment outside of the normal classroom for at least 2 hours per day. Ideally, these skill building lessons will not merely be worksheets distributed to students for independent, repetitive practice. And, they should not be merely row after row of exercises.

Intensive intervention should be designed to reteach concepts and skills, thus improving every student's mathematical understanding and procedures. Skill building lessons that are visual and require minimal amounts of reading enable students to work on their own.

" Teaching new mathematics standards to students is analogous to teaching students to swim: expecting students to instantly rise to the rigor of new standards, without bridging the gaps between the old and new standards, sets students up for failure."

Stepped out models and guided practice of strategies to help students bridge their skill gaps should be provided, before students practice independently. Manipulative activities and games are greatly useful in sustaining interest and engagement during this relearning stage. By following such a structure, students can learn the concepts, skills, and procedures they were lacking.

Strategic Intervention

Students at this level are struggling but still on grade-level. With sustained attention and guidance, a teacher can help lift a student back to the benchmark level without intensive intervention. The Diagnostic Assessment tables found in the Teacher Editions provide numerous options to instruct struggling students.

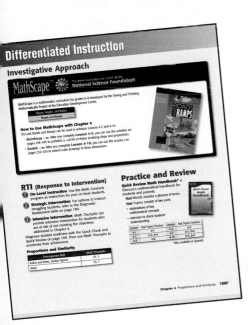

Benchmark and Above-Level Students

At the same time, students who do have the required prerequisite skills need to be appropriately challenged so they are continually improving their mathematical understanding and do not become bored. For students who do have the necessary prerequisite skills to continue onto new math concepts, skill building activities are not the answer. These on level and advanced students benefit from activities providing a variety of math challenges and experiences they can work on independently. Whenever possible, the teacher should strive to give these students dedicated time as well. Students should be asked higher order thinking questions about the concepts (horizontal) and be challenged with the next grade level's curriculum (vertical).

Summary

Because of the sequential nature of mathematics, when students have deficiencies in their understanding of previous areas of emphasis, it becomes extremely difficult for them to understand new topics that are based on those understandings. Teachers can use entry-level tests, especially when the standards expected of the students have become more rigorous, and then use the results to inform instruction. "It is important that teachers go beyond simply calculating a score to examine each child's response to each item" (Cathcart, 2000). Students and teachers need to work together to build skills that are lacking by reteaching necessary prerequisite skills. A solid mathematics program will provide entry-level tests and skill

building activities based on the test items to enable students to bridge the gaps so they can move forward successfully.

References

Cathcart, W. George, Yvonne M. Pothier, James H. Vance, and Nadine S. Bezuk. Learning Mathematics in Elementary and Middle Schools. Columbus: Ohio: Prentice Hall, 2000.

Selby, Alan M. "Mathematics from Primary School to College." Mathematics Curriculum Notes, Volume 1B, August 1997.

Van De Walle, John. Elementary and Middle School Mathematics: Teaching Developmentally. White Plains, NY: Addison Wesley Longman, Inc., 1997.

Robyn Silbey is a 30-plus year veteran of Montgomery County Public Schools in Maryland, currently working as a math content coach. She holds an M.S. in Elementary Mathematics Education from McDaniel College and a B.S. in Elementary Education from the University of Maryland. Robyn is a national consultant and serves as a teacher consultant in the Teaching Training Corps for the U.S. Department of Education.

Research Bibliography

Selected Research Bibliography
The following resources represent a sample of the research used as the foundation for Glencoe's *Math Connects* program.

General
Bransford, J. D., A. L. Brown, R. R. Cocking, et al. *How People Learn: Brain, Mind, Experience, and School.* Washington, DC: National Academy Press, 2000. 24.

Edwards, Edgar L., Jr., ed. *Algebra for Everyone.* Reston, VA: NCTM, 1990.

Grouws, Douglas A. ed. *Handbook of Research on Mathematics Teaching.* New York: Maxwell Macmillan, 1992.

Kloosterman, P. and Gainey, P. H. "Students' Thinking: Middle Grades Mathematics." *Research Ideas for the Classroom: Middle Grades Mathematics.* Reston: National Council of Teachers of Mathematics, 1993. 10.

National Research Council. *Adding It Up: Helping Children Learn Mathmatics.* J. Kilpatrick, J. Swafford, and B. Findell, eds. Washington: National Academy Press, 2001.

Selby, Alan M. "Mathematics from Primary School to College." *Mathematics Curriculum Notes* 1B (Aug 1997).

Van De Walle, John. *Elementary and Middle School Mathematics: Teaching Developmentally.* White Plains: Addison Wesley Longman, Inc., 1997.

Vygotsky, L. *Thought and Language.* Cambridge: MIT Press, 1962.

Assessment
Black, Paul and Dylan William. "Inside the Black Box: Raising Standards through Classroom Assessment." *Phi Delta Kappan* (Oct 1998): 139–48.

Nicholls, J. G. "Achievement Motivations: Conceptions of Ability, Subjective Experience, Task Choice, and Performance." *Psychological Review* 91: 328–46.

Differentiated Instruction
Alexander, P. A. "Training analogical reasoning Skills in the Gifted." *Roeper Review* 6:4 (1984): 191–193.

Banks, J. A. *Cultural Diversity and Education: Foundations, Curriculum and Teaching.* 4th ed. *Multiethnic Education: Theory and Practice.* Boston: Allyn and Bacon, 2001.

Banks, James and Cherry Banks. *Multicultural Education: Issues and Perspectives.* 2nd ed. Boston: Allyn and Bacon, 1993.

Baroody, Arthur J. "An Investigative Approach to the Mathematics Instruction of Children Classified as Learning Disabled." *Cognitive Approaches to Learning Disabilities.* Ed. D. Kim Reid, Wayne P. Hresko, and H. Lee Swanson. Austin: Pro-Ed, 1996. 547–615.

Brimijoin, K., E. Marquisee, and C. Tomlinson. "Using Data to Differentiate Instruction." *Educational Leadership* 60:5 (Feb 2003): 70–72.

Fisher, D. and C. H. Kennedy. "Differentiated Instruction for Diverse Middle School Students." *Inclusive Middle School.* Baltimore: Paul H. Brookes, 2001.

Stevenson, H. W. and J. W. Stigler. *The Learning Gap.* New York: Simon & Schuster, 1992.

Tomlinson, C. "Quality Curriculum and Instruction for Highly Able Students." *Theory into Practice* 44:2 (2005): 160–166.

Tomlinson, C. "The Mobius Effect: Addressing Learner Variance in Schools." *Journal of Learning Disabilities* 37:6 (2004): 516–524.

Tomlinson, C. A., C. Brighton, H. Hertberg, C. M. Callahan, T. R. Moon, K. Brimijoin, L. A. Conover, and T. Reynolds. "Differentiating Instruction in Response to Student Readiness, Interest, and Learning Profile in Academically Diverse Classroom: A Review of Literature." *Journal for the Education of the Gifted* 27 (2003): 119–145.

English Learners
Mohan, B. "The Second Language as a Medium of Learning." *English as a second language in the mainstream.* Eds. B. Mohan, C. Leung, and C. Davison. Harlow: Longman, 2001. 107–126.

Snow, M. A., M. Met, and F.Genesee. "A Conceptual Framework for the Integration of Language and Content in Second/Foreign Language Instruction." *TESOL Quarterly* 23:2 (1989): 201–217.

Swain, M. "Integrating Language and Content in Immersion Classrooms: Research Perspectives." *The Canadian Modern Language Review* 52:4 (1996): 529–548.

Foldables™/Graphic Organizers
Alvermann, D. E. and P. R. Boothby. "Children's Transfer of Graphic Organizer Instruction." *Reading Psychology* 7:2 (1986): 87–100.

Darch, C. B., D. W. Carnine, and E. J. Kameenui. "The Role of Graphic Organizers and Social Structure in Content Area Instruction." *Journal of Reading Behavior* 18:4 (1986): 275–295.

Gerlic, I. and N. Jausovec. "Multimedia: Differences in Cognitive Processes Observed with EEG." *Educational Technology Research and Development* 47:3 (1999): 5–14.

Research Bibliography

Horton, S. V., T. C. Lovitt, and D. Bergerud. "The Effectiveness of Graphic Organizers for Three Classifications of Secondary Students in Content Area Classes." *Journal of Learning Disabilities* 23:1 (1990): 12–22.

Mayer, R.E. "Can Advance Organizers Influence Meaningful Learning?" *Review of Educational Research* 49 (1979): 371–383

Mayer, R.E. "Models of understanding." *Review of Educational Research* 59:1 (1989): 43–64.

Robinson, D. H. and D. A. Kiewra. "Visual Argument: Graphic Organizers are Superior to Outlines in Improving Learning from Text." *Journal of Educational Psychology* 87:3 (1996): 455–467.

Instructional Strategies

Behr, M. J. and T. R. Post. "Teaching Rational Number and Decimal Concepts." *Teaching Mathematics in Grades K–8: Research Based Methods.* Boston: Allyn and Bacon, 1992.

Carpenter, T. P., E. Fennema, M. L. Franke, L. Levi, and S.E. Empson. *Children's Mathematics: Cognitively Guided Instruction.* Westport: Heinemann, 1999.

Carpenter, T. P. and R. Lehrer. (1999). "Teaching and Learning Mathematics with Understanding." Eds. E. Fennema and T. A. Romberg. *Mathematics Classrooms that Promote Understanding.* Mahwah: Lawrence Erlbaum, 1999. 19–32.

Cohen, E. and J. Benton. "Making Groupwork Work." *American Educator* 12:3 (1988): 10–17, 45–46.

Crawford, M. and M. Witte. "Strategies for Mathematics: Teaching in Context." *Educational Leadership.* Vol. 57. ASCD, Nov 1999.

Hiebert, J., T. P. Carpenter, E. Fennema, K. C. Fuson, H. Murray, A. Olivier, P. Human, and D. Wearner. *Making Sense: Teaching and Learning Mathematics with Understanding.* Portsmouth: Heinemann, 1997.

Jones, B., A. Palincsar, D. Ogle, and E. Carr. *Strategic Teaching and Learning: Cognitive Instruction in the Content Areas.* Alexandria: Association for Supervision and Curriculum Development, 1987.

Kintsch, W. "On Modeling Comprehension." *Educational Psychologist* 1 (1979): 3–14.

Mason, L. "Analogy, Meta-conceptual Awareness and Conceptual Change: A Classroom Study." *Educational Studies* 20:2 (1995): 267–291.

Mason, L. "Cognitive and Metacognitive Aspects in Conceptual Change by Analogy." *Instructional Science* 22:3 (1994): 157–187.

Means, B., C. Chelener, and M. Knapp. *Teaching Advanced Skills to At-Risk Students.* Dale Seymour Publications, 1991.

Medin, D., R. L. Goldstone, and A. B. Markman. "Comparison and Choice: Relationship between Similarity Processes and Decision Processes." *Psychonomic Bulletin & Review* 2:1 (1995): 1–19.

Newby, T J., P. A. Ertmer, and D. A. Stepich. "Instructional Analogies and the Learning of Concepts." *Educational Technology Research and Development* 43:1 (1995): 5–18.

Palincsar, A.S. and A. L. Brown. "Reciprocal Teaching of Comprehension Fostering and Comprehension Monitoring Activities." *Cognition and Instruction* 1:2 (1984): 117–175.

Ripoll, T. "Why This Made Me Think of That." *Thinking and Reasoning* 4:1 (1999): 15–43.

Rosenshine, B. and C. C. Meister. "Reciprocal Teaching: A Review of the Research." *Review of Educational Research* 64:4 (1994): 479–530.

Rosenshine, B., C. Meister, and S. Chapman. "Teaching Students to Generate Questions: A Review of the Intervention Studies." *Review of Educational Research* 66:2 (1996): 181–221.

Ross, B.H. "This is Like That: The Use of Earlier Problems and the Separation of Similarity Effects." *Journal of Experimental Psychology* 13:4 (1987): 629–639.

Wood, T. and T. Turner-Vorbeck. "Extending the Conception of Mathematics Teaching." Eds. T. Wood, B. S. Nelson, and J. Warfield. *Beyond Classical Pedagogy: Teaching Elementary School Mathematics.* Mahwah: Lawrence Eribaum Associates, 2001. 185–208.

Mathematical Content

Anghileri, J. and D. C. Johnson. "Arithmetic Operations on Whole Numbers: Multiplication and Division." *Teaching Mathematics in Grades K–8.* Boston: Allyn and Bacon, 1992. 157–200.

Brodie, J.P. *Constructing Ideas About Large Numbers.* Creative Publications, 1995.

Cathcart, W., George, Y. Pothier, and R. B. Ashlock. *Error Patterns in Computation.* 7th Ed. Columbus: Merrill, 1998.

Clements, D. *Learning and Teaching Measurement.* Ralston: NCTM, 2003.

Franco, B., et al. *Understanding Geometry.* Great Source Education Group, 1998.

Hoffer, A. R. and S. A. K. Hoffer. "Ratios and Proportional Thinking." *Teaching Mathematics in Grades K–8: Research Based Methods.* Boston: Allyn and Bacon, 1992.

Kaput, J. and J. E. Sims-Knight. "Errors in Translations to Algebraic Equations: Roots and Implications." *Focus on Learning Problems in Mathematics* 5:3 (1983): 63–78.

Lamon, S. *Teaching Fractions and Ratios for Understanding.* Mahwah: Lawrence Erlbaum Associates, 1999.

Piccirilli, R. *Mental Math: Computation Activities for Anytime.* Scholastic Books, 1996.

Rathmell, Edward C. "Using Thinking Strategies to Teach the Basic Facts." *Developing Computational Skills.* Ed. Marilyn N. Suydam. Reston: NCTM, 1978.

Trafton, P. and D. Thiesen. *Learning through Problems: Number Sense and Computational Strategies: A Resource for Teachers.* Heinemann, 1999.

Problem Solving

Chen, Z. "Children's Analogical Problem Solving: The Effects of Superficial, Structural, and Procedural Similarities." *Journal of Experimental Child Psychology* 62:3 (1996): 410–431.

Chen, Z. "Schema Induction in Children's Analogical Problem Solving." *Journal of Educational Psychology* 91:4 (1999): 703–715.

Duncker, K. "On problem-solving (L.S. Less, Trans.)." *Psychological Monographs* (1945): 58, 270.

English, L.D. "Children's Reasoning in Classifying and Solving Computational Word Problems." Ed. L.D. English. *Mathematical Reasoning: Analogies, Metaphors and Images.* Mahwah: Lawrence Erlbaum, 1997. 191–220.

Gick, M. L. and K. J. Holyoak. "Analogical Problem Solving." *Cognitive Psychology* 12 (1980): 306–355.

Charles, R. I. and F. K. Lester, Jr. "An Evaluation of a Process Oriented Mathematical Problem-Solving Instructional Program in Grades 5 and 7." *Journal for Research in Mathematics Education* 15:1 (1984): 15–34.

Hiebert, J. "Signposts for Teaching Mathematics through Problem Solving." Eds. F. K. Lester, Jr. and R. I. Charles. *Teaching Mathematics through Problem Solving.* Reston: National Council of Teachers of Mathematics, 2003. 53–61.

Polya, G. *How to Solve It: A New Aspect of Mathematical Method.* 2nd Ed. Princeton: Princeton University Press, 1957.

Stanic, G. M. A. and J. Kilpatrick. "Historical Perspectives on Problem Solving in the mathematics Curriculum." Eds. R. I. Charles and E. A. Silver. *The Teaching and Assessing of Mathematical Problem Solving.* Reston: National Council of Teacher of Mathematics, 1989. 1–22.

Steen, L. A. and S. L. Forman. "Mathematics for Work and Life." Ed. Iris M. Carl. *Prospects for School Mathematics; Seventy-Five years of Progress.* Reston: National Council of Teachers of Mathematics, 1995. 221.

Suydam, M.N. "Untangling Clues from Research on Problem Solving." Eds. S. Krulik and R. E. Reys. *Problem Solving in School Mathematics: 1980 Yearbook.* Reston: National Council of Teachers of Mathematics, 1980. 43.

Reading & Writing

Armbruster, B. B. "Considerate Texts." Eds. D. Lapp, J. Flood, and N. Farnan. *Content Area Reading and Learning: Instructional Strategies.* Needham Heights: Allyn & Bacon, 1996. 47–57.

Armbruster, B. B., T. H. Anderson, and J. Ostertag. "Does Text Structure/Summarization Instruction Facilitate Learning from Expository Text?" *Reading Research Quarterly* 22:3 (1987): 331–346.

Baumann, J. F. and E. J. Kameenui. "Research on Vocabulary Instruction: Ode to Voltaire." Eds. J. Flood, J. M. Jensen, D. Lapp, and J. R. Squire. *Handbook on Teaching the English Language Arts.* New York: Macmillan, 1991.

Blachowicz, C. L. Z. "Making Connections: Alternatives to the Vocabulary Notebook." *Journal of Reading* 29:2 (1986): 643–649.

Burton, Leone and Candia Morgan. "Mathematicians Writing." *Journal for Research in Mathematics Education* 31:4 (2000).

Carr, E. and D. Ogle. "K-W-L Plus: A Strategy for Comprehension and Summarization." *Journal of Reading* 30 (1987): 626–631.

Davey, B. "Using Textbook Activity Guides to Help Students Learn from Textbooks." *Journal of Reading* 29 (1986): 489–494.

Eanet, M. and A. Manzo. "R.E.A.P.--A Strategy for Improving Reading/Writing Study Skills." *Journal for Reading* 19 (1976): 647–652.

Fielding, L. G. and P. D. Pearson. "Synthesis of Research: Reading Comprehension: What Works." *Educational Leadership* 51:5 (1994): 62–67.

Golembo, Vadim. "Writing a PEMDAS Story" *Mathematics Teaching in the Middle School* 5:9 (2000).

Hoffman, J. "Critical Reading/Thinking Across the Curriculum: Using I-Charts to Support Learning." *Language Arts* 69 (1992): 121–127.

Manzo, A. "The ReQuest Procedure." *Journal of Reading* 13 (1969): 23–26.

Martin, C. E., M. A. Martin, and D. G. O'Brien. "Spawning Ideas for Writing in the Content Area." *Reading World* 11 (1984): 11–15.

Marzano, R. J. "Building Background Knowledge for Academic Achievement: Research on What Works in Schools." (2004).

McKeown, M., I. Beck, G. Sinatra, and J. Loxterman. "The Contribution of Prior Knowledge and Coherent Text to Comprehension." *Reading Research Quarterly* 27 (1992): 79–93.

Nagy, W. "On the Role of Context in First- and Second-language Vocabulary Learning." Eds. N. Schmitt and M. McCarthy. *Vocabulary: Description, Acquisition, and Pedagogy.* Cambridge, UK: Cambridge University Press, 1997. 64–83.

Nagy, W. and P. Herman. "Breadth and Depth of Vocabulary Knowledge: Implication for Acquisition and Instruction." Eds. M. McKeown and M. Curties. *The Nature of Vocabulary Acquisition.* Hillsdale: Erlbaum, 1987.

Palinscar, A. S. and A. Brown. "Interactive Teaching to Promote Independent Learning from Text." *Reading Teacher* 39:8 (1986): 771–777.

Raphael, T. and P. D. Pearson. *The Effect of Metacognitive Awareness Training on Children's Question Answering Behavior.* Tech. Report 238. Urbana: Center for the Study of Reading, 1982.

Raphael, T. "Teaching Learners about Sources of Information for Answering Comprehension Questions." *Journal of Reading* 27 (1984): 303–311.

Research Bibliography

Siegel, M., R. Borasi, J. M. Fonzi, L. G. Sandridge, and
    C. Smith. "Using Reading to Construct Mathematical
    Meaning." Ed. P. C. Elliot. *Communication in
    Mathematics, K–12 and Beyond: 1996 Yearbook*.
    Reston: National Council of Teachers of Mathematics,
    1996. 74.
Whitin, D. J. and P. E. Whitin. "The 'Write' Way to
    Mathematical Understanding." Ed. Lorna J. Morrow.
    *Teaching and Learning of Algorithms in School
    Mathematics*. Reston: National Council of Teachers
    of Mathematics, Inc., 1998. 161–169.

Research Bibliography